BEFORE I MADE HISTORY™

Give Me a Sign, Helen Keller!

Give Me a Sign, Helen Keller!

by Peter and Connie Roop

SCHOLASTIC INC.

New York   Toronto   London   Auckland   Sydney
Mexico City   New Delhi   Hong Kong   Buenos Aires

ISBN 0-439-55444-6

Text copyright © 2004 by Peter and Connie Roop.
Illustrations copyright © 2004 by Scholastic Inc.
All rights reserved. Published by Scholastic Inc.
SCHOLASTIC and associated logos are trademarks and/or
registered trademarks of Scholastic Inc.

12 11   8 9/0

Printed in the U.S.A.   40
First printing, March 2004

For Amy, whose humor and compassion
touch the world! Bingo!

Contents

Introduction

Helen Keller is famous. She could not see or hear. Do you know how she lost her sight and hearing?

Helen spent most of her life blind and deaf. Do you know that Helen Keller learned to read, write, and talk?

When she was young, Helen had many temper tantrums. Do you know why?

When she was six years old, Helen didn't know any words. Do you know how she learned to communicate?

Helen's teacher was Anne Sullivan. Do you know that Anne had been blind?

Helen talked with her hands and learned how to write the letters of the alphabet. Do you know how she did this?

Helen was introduced to many famous people. Do you know how many United States presidents she met?

Helen didn't let her blindness and deafness stop her from enjoying the world. Do you know she helped other children who were blind and deaf?

Helen loved to be outside. Do you know what her favorite activities were?

Helen worked hard to go to college. Do you know she was the first person who was blind and deaf to graduate from an American college?

Helen loved to write. Do you know she wrote a book about her life when she was still in college?

Helen enjoyed sharing her story. Do you know Helen gave speeches?

The answers to these questions lie in who Helen Keller was as a child and as a young woman. This book is about Helen Keller before she made history.

1

Helen Is Born

June 27, 1880, was a happy day for Kate and Arthur Keller. That day, Helen, their first daughter, was born in their home in Tuscumbia, Alabama.

The Kellers named their home Ivy Green for the beautiful English ivy covering the house, trees, and nearby fences. Bees buzzed around the rainbow of flowers that Mrs. Keller planted in her garden. A servant pumped cool water from the well in the yard. Dogs slept in the summer sun. Turkeys scratched the ground searching for food. Captain Keller's cotton plants grew green and tall.

Inside Ivy Green, Helen Keller cried. Her mother gently rocked her to sleep. One day, Helen Keller would be famous throughout the world as a girl who was blind and deaf but could read, write, and give speeches. Helen would meet kings, queens, and presidents. She would laugh with authors, poets, and artists. Helen would even have a ship, the *Helen Keller*, named after her.

All of this lay in the future for Helen Keller. For now, she was her parents' pride. Later, Helen wrote, "I came, I saw, I conquered as the first baby in the family always does."

Helen's father had been a Confederate captain in the Civil War. When the war ended, Captain Keller returned to Ivy Green. He grew cotton and ran his newspaper, *The Northern Alabamian*. Captain Keller had been married before and had two sons, James and Frank, but his first wife had died.

Then he married Kate Adams, who would be Helen's mother. Captain Keller built a small wooden house near Ivy Green where he entertained his hunting friends. The Kellers called it the Little House. The Little House was covered with vines, climbing yellow roses, and sweet-smelling honeysuckle. One day, this beautiful little house would change Helen's life.

As a baby, Helen was dressed in long white gowns. She was bright and curious. Before long, Helen was crawling around, exploring her world. Helen eagerly watched her family. When someone did something, Helen copied it.

When Helen was six months old, she already knew some words. She said, "How d'ye," when she saw someone. One day, she surprised her parents and said, "Tea, tea, tea." When she was thirsty, Helen asked for "wah-wah," her special word for water.

When she was one year old, Helen discovered she could walk. Her mother was holding Helen in her lap when Helen saw shadows of leaves on the floor. She slid from her mother's lap and toddled toward the shadows. Suddenly, Helen realized that no one was holding her, and she fell down. Mrs. Keller comforted her surprised daughter.

Now that she could walk, Helen explored

more of her world. One of her favorite things to do was to greet her father at the gate when he returned home from work. Every day, Captain Keller picked Helen up, hugged her, and asked, "What has my little woman been doing today?" Captain Keller knew that the very active Helen had done many things.

2
Helen Becomes Blind and Deaf

In February 1882, when Helen was nineteen months old, she had a high fever. The Kellers called the doctor. He didn't think Helen would live. Mrs. Keller bathed Helen to keep the fever down. She soothed Helen as she tossed and turned in her crib. Mrs. Keller didn't notice that Helen often turned her aching eyes away from the bright sunlight coming through her window.

One day, Helen's fever left as mysteriously as it had come. Captain and Mrs. Keller were overjoyed at Helen's recovery. But they were also puzzled. Helen didn't respond when they said her name. She didn't flinch when they clapped their hands loudly. She didn't close her eyes when her mother bathed her.

Slowly, the Kellers understood. The terrible fever had robbed Helen of her sight and hearing. Helen Keller was blind and deaf! Later, Helen wrote, "The cruel fever had taken my sight and hearing; taken all the light and music and gladness out of my little life." Helen's world was totally dark and absolutely silent.

Helen didn't understand what had happened. She didn't understand why she couldn't see or hear. She clung to her mother's dress as she did her household chores. She sat in her mother's lap while her mother held her tenderly.

Helen's mind and hands grew restless. She touched and smelled things, trying to understand what they were. She felt her mother's lips. She touched her father's newspaper. She petted Belle, their dog. She hugged her doll. She played with keys. She smelled flowers and food.

Helen wanted to let her family know her

needs, so she made simple signs to communicate. When she shook her head, Helen meant "No." When she nodded her head, she meant "Yes." When Helen pulled on someone's clothes, she meant "Come." When she pushed someone away, she meant "Go."

When Helen wanted bread, she pretended to slice a loaf of bread and put butter on it. When Helen wanted ice cream, she pretended to crank the ice-cream churn handle, and she shivered as though she were cold. When she wanted cake, Helen acted like she was stirring a bowl of cake batter.

Helen could tell when her mother was going out by the clothes she wore. Helen begged to go with her. Often, her mother took Helen along to give her more experiences in the world beyond Ivy Green. Helen especially liked going into town to visit her cousins.

Mrs. Keller showed great patience with Helen, trying to help her as best as she could. Her father did everything he could to make Helen happy. But both parents worried about their daughter.

Helen's dark, quiet world made her angry. She threw temper tantrums if she didn't get her way. She kicked and screamed until she was worn out. Helen felt trapped in her silent world, and she didn't know how to get out.

Still, Helen learned many things. Her mother hand-signaled things she needed. Helen would go upstairs to get what her mother wanted, feeling her way along the walls and up the stairs. When Helen was five years old, she learned how to fold laundry. She knew which clothes were hers, and she knew where to put them.

Helen enjoyed meeting people. When guests put on their coats to leave, she always waved good-bye. Helen's world was dark and quiet, but she was rarely lonely.

3
Helen's World

Helen's closest companion was Martha Washington, an African-American girl who was two years older than Helen. Martha's mother cooked for the Kellers. Martha understood Helen's signs and usually did what Helen wanted to do. But when she didn't, Helen fought her.

Helen was strong and always wanted her way. Like the Kellers, Martha gave in to Helen so that Helen wouldn't throw temper tantrums. But Martha and Helen had fun, too. They spent many hours in the kitchen helping Martha's mother cook. They baked bread and cakes. They churned the ice-cream machine to make ice cream. They ground coffee. They fed the turkeys pecking in the yard. Helen especially enjoyed this because the tame turkeys ate out of her hand.

One day when she was five years old, Helen was holding a tomato in her hand. A big turkey grabbed the tomato and gobbled it down.

Helen was very naughty sometimes. She smelled a cake baking. This gave her an idea! The turkey took Helen's tomato and ate it, so she would take the cake and eat it. When the cook wasn't looking, Helen and Martha grabbed the cake and ran to a woodpile. There they ate the whole cake. Helen did not get into trouble, but she did get very sick from all that cake!

One hot July day in 1886, Helen and Martha were cutting out paper dolls. They grew tired of cutting paper and used the scissors to cut their shoelaces instead. Then they cut all the leaves off the honeysuckle vine. Helen cut off some of Martha's hair. Martha cut off one of Helen's curls. Martha was just getting ready to cut them all off when Mrs. Keller stopped her.

Helen loved to look for nests in the grass. To show Martha what she wanted to do, Helen held her hands together and put them on the ground. This was Helen's sign for nest. When they found a nest, Helen took all the eggs. She didn't trust Martha to carry them because she thought Martha might trip and fall and break the eggs.

Helen enjoyed the activity in the farmyard. The girls explored the shed where the corn was stored. They wandered in the stable where the horses and mules were kept. They fed hay to the animals. Helen helped milk the cows, too. Although Helen's world was dark and quiet, her hands and active fingers helped her to learn about her surroundings.

Sometimes Martha did not want to play with Helen, especially when Helen was being mean and bossy. Helen would turn her attention to their dog, Belle. Belle was an old hunting dog who liked to sleep. Belle would move away from Helen. Helen would catch Belle and hand-signal to her what she wanted to do. Belle didn't understand Helen's signs

and struggled to get free. Finally, Helen would get bored and leave Belle alone.

Helen especially enjoyed Christmas, though she had no idea what the holiday was about. She liked the different smells filling the house. She and Martha helped with the Christmas cooking. They ground spices. They mixed cake batter and licked the spoons. They picked over the raisins, selecting the best ones for pies, puddings, and popping into their mouths. Helen hung her stocking because everyone else did. In the morning, she was surprised to find it filled with presents.

One day, Helen had a terrible accident. She spilled water on her apron, so she spread the apron on the floor in front of the fire. Helen grew impatient waiting for it to dry. Unable to see exactly where the fire was, Helen held the apron over the flames. It caught fire. The flames spread to Helen's dress. Helen screamed. Viny, a family helper, heard Helen's cries. She covered her with a blanket and put out the flames. Helen's hands and hair were burned, and she was badly frightened.

4
Helen Takes a Train Ride

Helen's everyday world always seemed the same. She woke, played, ate, helped, and slept. But Helen had no idea what the world was really like. When she got frustrated, Helen burst into longer, angrier tantrums.

She behaved like a wild animal, taking food off other people's plates. Helen hit and pinched people when she didn't get her way. In 1885, when Helen was five years old, her world changed. That year, Helen's sister, Mildred, was born. Helen was upset now that her mother paid so much attention to the new baby. Helen grew very jealous of Mildred.

One day, Mildred was sleeping in her cradle. Mildred's cradle used to be for Helen's doll, Nancy. That day, Helen discovered Mildred in the cradle and got very angry. Helen grabbed the cradle and turned it over!

Mildred fell out of her cradle. Fortunately, Mrs. Keller was nearby and caught Mildred before she hit the hard floor. Mrs. Keller was very upset. Helen could have killed her baby sister!

The Kellers wondered if Helen should be sent away to a special place for people who could not control themselves. The Kellers reached a decision after Helen was especially mean to her mother.

Helen had learned what keys were for. She went around locking and unlocking doors. One morning, her mother went into the pantry to get some food. Helen locked the pantry door behind her mother!

Mrs. Keller pounded on the door. Helen sat on the front porch steps, rocking and laughing. She felt her mother's pounding through vibrations in the floor. She felt the key in her apron pocket. Finally, after three hours, someone rescued Mrs. Keller. Something had to be done with Helen. But what?

The answer came in 1886, when Helen was six years old. Mrs. Keller was reading a book by Charles Dickens, a famous English author. Mr. Dickens had written about Laura Bridgman, a woman who was blind and deaf and who lived in Boston. Laura Bridgman was a student at the Perkins Institute, a school for people who were blind.

Mrs. Keller was fascinated with Laura's story. Laura was the first person in the world who had been taught to communicate with other people even though she was blind and deaf. Laura could read, write, and spell with her hands. Mrs. Keller wondered if Laura's teachers could help Helen.

Captain Keller, however, suggested that he take Helen to see Dr. Chisholm, an eye doctor in Baltimore. Captain Keller believed Dr. Chisholm might be able to help Helen regain her eyesight.

In the summer of 1886, Helen, Captain

Keller, and Helen's Aunt Ev rode the train to Baltimore. Helen enjoyed the adventure of riding on a train and having new experiences. She made friends with people on the train. One lady shared a box of seashells with Helen. Captain Keller made holes in the shells. Helen spent hours stringing her shells together.

Helen made friends with the train conductor. He let Helen walk through the train cars as he punched the passengers' tickets. When the conductor didn't need his ticket punch, he let Helen play with it. Helen spent many hours happily punching holes.

Aunt Ev made a doll out of towels for Helen to play with. The doll had no eyes, ears, nose, or mouth. Helen wanted her doll to have eyes. She tried "telling" Aunt Ev what she wanted. Aunt Ev didn't understand. Finally, Helen grabbed her aunt's cape and pulled off two buttons. Helen showed her aunt that she wanted the buttons for her doll's eyes. Aunt Ev understood and sewed the "eyes" on Helen's doll.

Even though Aunt Ev had to sew the two buttons back on her cape, she was happy that Helen was able to communicate with her. Helen's father was also very pleased with Helen's behavior on the trip. She didn't throw a single temper tantrum the whole way.

5
Helen Gets Help

Dr. Chisholm examined Helen's eyes. He told Captain Keller that Helen would always be blind. He suggested that they see Dr. Alexander Graham Bell in Washington, D.C. Dr. Bell was famous for inventing the telephone and for helping deaf children. Maybe Dr. Bell could help Helen hear.

Helen and Dr. Bell immediately liked each other. Helen sensed Dr. Bell's kind, caring concern for her. Dr. Bell "read" Helen's hand signals. He held Helen on his knee and let her play with his watch.

Dr. Bell examined Helen's ears. He told Captain Keller there was nothing he could do for Helen. He suggested that they see Mr.

Michael Anagnos who ran the Perkins Institute in Boston, the same place that Mrs. Keller had read about!

Instead of traveling to Boston, Captain Keller wrote to Mr. Anagnos. He told him about Helen's deafness and blindness. Captain Keller asked if he knew a teacher who would come to Tuscumbia, live with the Kellers, and teach Helen.

Finally, a letter arrived from the Perkins Institute. Yes, Mr. Anagnos knew a teacher who might be able to help Helen. She had once been blind, but nine operations had given her back much of her eyesight. This person was a student at Perkins, and she would be able to come to Tuscumbia in March of 1887. The teacher's name was Anne Sullivan, a name that would be forever linked with Helen Keller's name.

On March 3, 1887, Anne Sullivan stepped off the train in Tuscumbia. Mrs. Keller and her stepson James met Anne at the station. Anne enjoyed the beautiful wagon ride to Ivy

Green. Captain Keller greeted Anne and welcomed her with cheery words. Anne was eager to meet Helen.

"Where is Helen?" she asked.

Captain Keller said, "There she is. She has known all day that someone was expected, and she has been wild ever since her mother went to the station for you."

Helen was standing on the porch. Anne stepped onto the porch. Helen felt the vibration of Anne's footsteps. Helen ran into Anne with such force that Anne was almost knocked down. Helen's fingers flew over Anne's face. She touched Anne's eyes, nose, and mouth. She felt her hair. She touched Anne's dress. Helen grabbed Anne's bag and yanked it out of her arms. Later, Helen wrote, "The most important day I remember in all my life is the one on which my teacher, Anne Mansfield Sullivan, came to me."

Helen tried to open Anne's bag, but she couldn't. Helen felt for a keyhole. When she found it, Helen acted out turning a key. She pointed to Anne's bag. Before Anne could answer, Mrs. Keller told Helen with hand-signals that she should not touch Anne's bag anymore. Helen's face grew red. Mrs. Keller tried to take the bag out of Helen's hands. Helen grew even angrier.

Anne came to the rescue. She put her watch in Helen's hand. Helen calmed down. Then Helen took Anne upstairs to the bedroom she would use. Anne opened her bag. Helen searched for candy. She was disappointed when she didn't find any.

In the morning, Anne showed Helen her clothes trunk. Helen helped Anne unpack. Helen tried on Anne's bonnet. She stood in front of the mirror, turning her head one way, then another. Anne was surprised. Helen acted as though she saw herself in the mirror!

As Helen pulled things from the trunk, Anne studied her student. She saw that Helen was healthy and strong. She noticed that Helen was never still. Anne wrote that Helen was "here, there, everywhere. Her hands are in everything; but nothing holds her attention for long."

Anne was pleased that Helen was so curious and healthy. Anne was determined not to show any pity for Helen's deafness and blindness. But Anne wrote to a friend, "Dear child, her restless spirit gropes in the dark." Anne wondered how she could be let into Helen's world.

6

Helen's First Lessons

Helen found a doll in Anne's trunk. It was a present for Helen. The blind children at the Perkins Institute had made it. Laura Bridgman, the Perkins Institute student whom Mrs. Keller had read about, had sewn the doll's clothes.

Helen hugged her doll. She touched its eyes, nose, mouth, ears, and hair. She sniffed her doll. Helen pointed to the doll, to herself, and nodded her head. This was Helen's sign for "mine."

Anne thought it was time to teach Helen her first word. Anne slowly spelled d-o-l-l into Helen's hand using a hand-sign alphabet so Helen could feel the letters.

Helen was puzzled. She felt Anne's fingers

and hand. She liked this new game. Helen copied the letter shapes Anne had made. D-o-l-l. Helen pointed to her doll.

Helen had no idea what she was doing. She didn't connect the letters d-o-l-l with her new doll. Later, Helen wrote, "I was simply making my fingers go in monkey-like imitation."

Anne realized that Helen didn't even know that things had names. Anne took the doll away from Helen. She would give it back when Helen spelled d-o-l-l again.

Helen got angry. She tried to grab the doll away from Anne. Anne formed the letters d-o-l-l in Helen's hand again. Helen only grew angrier.

Anne forced Helen into a chair. Anne was determined to show she was in charge. Helen was equally determined to have her own way. Helen struggled. Anne held Helen in the chair until she was worn out. Anne decided to end this battle. She let Helen go, but held onto the doll. Anne ran downstairs for a piece of cake.

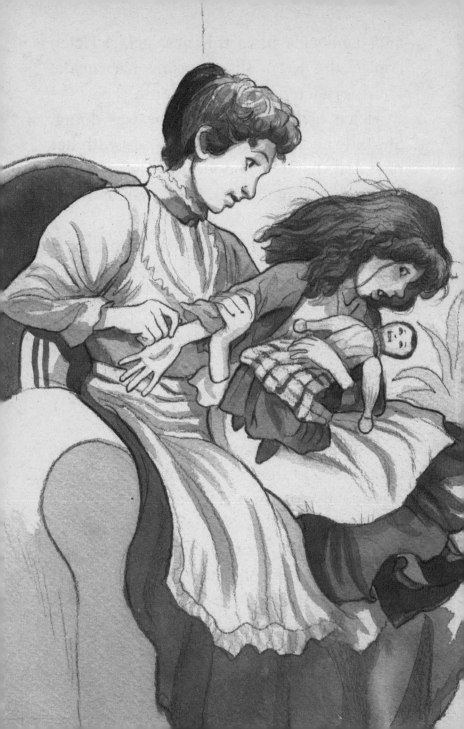

Anne held the cake in front of Helen so she could smell and touch it. She spelled c-a-k-e into Helen's hand. Helen tried to grab the cake, but Anne held it out of her reach. Anne spelled c-a-k-e again and patted Helen's hand. Helen copied Anne and spelled c-a-k-e. Anne gave Helen the cake. Helen gobbled up the cake. She didn't want Anne to take the cake away!

Anne showed Helen the doll again. She spelled d-o-l-l. Helen spelled d-o-l. Anne spelled the last *l* for Helen and gave her the doll. Helen ran downstairs with her doll. For the rest of the day, Helen refused to return to Anne's room.

Anne wondered how she could ever teach Helen if she acted wild and got so upset. Anne understood that Helen grew angry because she felt trapped in her silent, dark world. After three days with Helen, Anne wrote, "The greatest problem I shall have to solve is how to discipline and control her without breaking her spirit."

Anne decided to go slowly with Helen.

She wanted Helen to trust her. She wanted to win Helen's love. Anne knew she couldn't reach her student with force, but she needed Helen to obey her. Once that happened, Anne thought, she and Helen could unlock Helen's world.

7
Helen's Breakfast Battle

One morning, less than a week after Anne arrived, she and Helen had their biggest battle. At meals, Helen still walked around the table taking food off people's plates and stuffing it into her mouth.

Her parents let Helen have her way because they felt it was easier than having her throw a temper tantrum. This morning, however, Anne wouldn't let Helen take food off her plate. Anne had made up her mind. Helen would obey her, even if she did not obey anyone else.

Helen tried again to take food off Anne's plate. Anne pushed Helen's hand away. Helen tried again. Anne pushed again. Helen and Anne were in a battle of wills.

The Kellers were upset. They wanted Anne to let Helen do what she wanted. Anne told them Helen must obey her.

The Kellers left the dining room. Anne locked the door behind them. Anne began eating her breakfast. Helen lay on the floor, kicking and screaming.

Helen tried to pull Anne's chair out from under her. Anne kicked Helen's hand away. Helen pulled. Anne kicked. The struggle continued for thirty minutes.

Helen stood up and tried once again to grab food off Anne's plate. Anne pushed her hand away. Helen pinched Anne. Anne slapped Helen. Helen pinched. Anne slapped.

Helen walked around the table to see who else was in the room. Helen was surprised when she realized that everyone else was gone! Helen went to her seat and began eating with her fingers. Anne gave her a spoon. Helen threw it on the floor. Anne made Helen pick up the spoon, sit down, and eat with it. Helen gave in and ate her breakfast with the spoon.

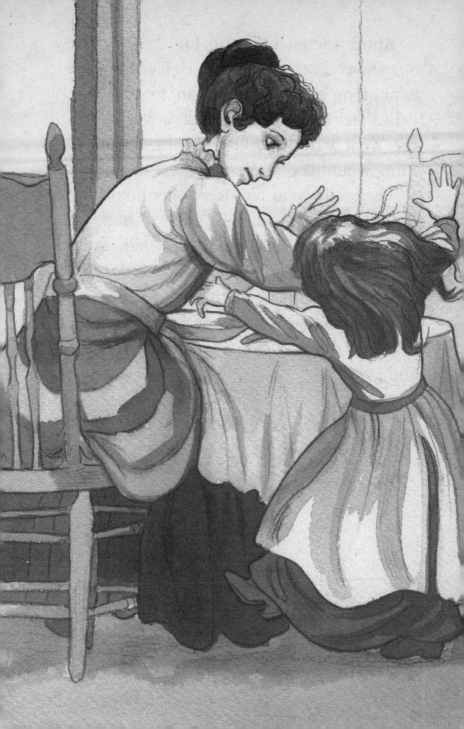

Anne wanted Helen to fold her napkin. She showed her what to do. Helen threw the napkin on the floor and ran to the door. When Helen discovered the door was locked, she went wild. She kicked. She screamed. Anne wouldn't give up.

The battle went on for another hour until Helen finally folded the napkin. Anne was tired, so she let Helen go outside. Anne went to her room and cried. She wrote a friend, "I suppose I shall have many such battles with the little woman before she learns the only essential things I can teach her, obedience and love."

8

Helen and Anne Move

That week, Anne realized that if Helen stayed in the house with her family, Anne wouldn't be able to reach her and teach her. Helen bossed everyone around. When Helen didn't get her way, she kicked and screamed. It was a fight just to get Helen to put on her shoes, comb her hair, or wash her hands.

Anne knew that as Helen grew older and bigger her tantrums would get wilder and more dangerous. Anne decided to take Helen away and teach her alone. But where could they go?

On their walks in the yard, Anne had seen the Little House that Captain Keller used for his hunting friends. Anne had an idea! She and Helen would live in the Little House.

Anne told the Kellers her idea, but Mrs. Keller didn't like it. She loved Helen and wanted her to live with her family. Captain Keller loved Helen, too, but he thought Anne's idea was a good one. Anne told them that if Helen lived in the Little House, the Kellers could see her every day without Helen even knowing it.

The Kellers finally agreed. Anne was excited. She thought the Little House was a "genuine bit of paradise." There was a large square room with a fireplace, a big bay window, and a small room. The front porch was covered with vines. There was a garden. So that Anne could give Helen her full attention, their food was cooked at Ivy Green and brought to the Little House.

But Helen hated the Little House! When she was taken there, she kicked and screamed until she was exhausted. When dinner came, Helen ate and played with her dolls. When it was bedtime, Helen put on her nightgown and lay down. Since there was only one bed, Helen had to share it with Anne. When Anne climbed into the bed, Helen leaped out and wouldn't get back in.

Anne didn't want Helen to catch a cold, so she insisted that Helen get in bed. Helen refused. Anne and Helen battled for two hours! Anne was surprised at Helen's strength and endurance.

Anne wouldn't give up. Finally, she wore Helen out. Helen got into bed. Anne gently covered her up and slept in a chair.

In the morning, Helen was homesick. She went to the door and waited for her mother. Mrs. Keller didn't come, so Helen played with her dolls.

Anne took Helen into the garden. Helen knew where she was by touching the hedges. She made her signs for mother, father, and brother. Anne taught Helen to hand spell more words. She taught her *pin, hat, cup, sit, stand, walk, mug,* and *milk.* Helen copied Anne's hand spelling, but she still didn't know what the words meant.

Anne knew this because one day Captain Keller brought over Belle. Helen smelled

Belle and hugged the dog. Helen spelled d-o-l-l into Belle's paw. Hand spelling was just a game to Helen, a game that she could play with Belle!

Anne decided she would be patient. She would teach Helen whenever she had a chance. They spent a great deal of time outside. Helen touched and smelled trees and flowers. She played in the dirt. One morning, Helen dug a hole and planted her doll. She signed to Anne that she wanted the doll to grow up tall like Anne.

Helen's fingers were always active, so Anne taught her how to knit. Helen learned quickly. She knitted a washcloth for her mother and an apron for her doll. Sometimes Helen played by herself, and other times Martha joined her. Anne, Martha, and Helen often visited the horses, mules, and cows in the stable. They fed the turkeys and hunted for eggs. When the weather was especially nice, Anne and Helen went for buggy rides. They stopped to see Helen's cousins. After dinner, Anne and Helen played games until eight o'clock, when it was bedtime. Each day, Helen trusted Anne more and more. She even let Anne share her bed so Anne didn't have to sleep on the chair anymore.

By April 1, 1887, Helen could hand spell twenty-nine words. But she still didn't know what the words meant. Then, on April 5, Helen's dark world suddenly brightened.

9

Helen Unlocks Her World

Helen didn't understand what m-u-g and m-i-l-k meant. When she spelled them, she made the motion for drinking something. Anne had an idea. She would take Helen to the water pump and spell m-u-g and w-a-t-e-r.

Helen held her mug under the faucet while Anne pumped the handle with one hand. With her other hand, Anne spelled w-a-t-e-r on Helen's palm. Suddenly, Helen dropped the mug, held her hand under the cold water, and spelled w-a-t-e-r over and over.

Helen Keller understood words! She understood that things have names! Anne said, "A new light came into her face."

Helen wrote, "I knew then that w-a-t-e-r meant the wonderful cool something that was flowing over my hand. That living word awakened my soul, gave it light, hope, joy, set it free!"

After that, Helen had to know the words for everything: pump, grass, trees, flowers. Before bed, Helen had learned how to spell thirty new words, like *door, open, shut, give, come, go, baby, mother, father,* and *sister.* But one word Helen learned that wonderful day was more important than any other.

Helen pointed to Anne and asked her name. Anne eagerly spelled t-e-a-c-h-e-r into Helen's hand. Helen spelled t-e-a-c-h-e-r. Anne was named Teacher. For the rest of their lives together, Anne was always Teacher.

That night, Helen hugged Anne for the very first time. Anne said, "I thought my heart would burst, so full was it of joy." Anne spelled into Helen's eager hands the sights, sounds, smells, tastes, and names of Ivy Green. Words were the keys Anne Sullivan used to unlock Helen Keller's world. Each

46

day, Helen learned new and more difficult words.

Helen and Anne spent hours inside and outside. Anne made maps in clay for Helen to feel mountains, rivers, valleys, and volcanoes. Helen learned how plants grew and how bees made honey. She kept tadpoles to learn how they grew into frogs. She touched fossils and learned about dinosaurs. Helen had a pet bird named Little Tim who hopped onto her fingers. Anne took Helen to a circus. Helen shook hands with a bear, petted a giraffe, cuddled a lion cub, and even rode an elephant! Soon, Helen knew how to spell more than four hundred words.

Just after Helen's seventh birthday, on June 28, 1887, Anne taught Helen how to read special books written in Braille for blind people. The raised dots in the Braille books stood for letters. Helen could feel Braille and read the words. Helen became a lifelong reader.

Anne taught Helen how to write. Helen used a board with special lines she could feel so she could keep her letters straight. Helen held a pencil in her right hand. She used her left hand to shape the letters. Helen wrote her first letter to her cousin Anna. Helen wrote,

helenwriteannageorgewillgivehelenapple

Helen didn't know what capital letters and periods were, but she would learn.

That Christmas, Helen finally understood what the celebration was all about. She even wrote Santa Claus a thank-you letter!

10
Helen Makes History

As Helen mastered spelling, reading, and writing, she wanted to learn even more words. The Kellers and Anne decided that Helen needed experiences beyond Ivy Green. Anne suggested taking Helen to Boston. Just before Helen turned eight years old, Anne and Helen journeyed to Boston. There, at the Perkins Institute, Helen met girls who were blind. She met Mr. Anagnos, who had sent Anne to be her teacher. And she met Laura Bridgman, who was such an inspiration.

Anne took Helen to the ocean. Helen jumped for joy in the waves. Anne laughed when Helen asked, "Who put the salt in the water?" Helen's world grew bigger and bigger every day.

People learned about the amazing Helen Keller, the girl who was blind and deaf but could read and write. Newspapers wrote stories about her. She was called "the wonder girl," "a marvel," and "a miracle."

When she was nine years old, Helen was determined to learn how to speak. For years, Helen practiced and practiced until she could finally talk. Sometimes it was hard to understand Helen because she didn't know how words sounded. She only knew how they felt when she used her vocal cords.

Helen studied hard with Anne and at school. She learned how to read and write German, French, and Greek. She struggled with math, but she worked hard to understand it. She learned science, history, and geography.

Helen decided to go to college. She studied extremely hard and passed the test for Radcliffe College. In the fall of 1900, when she was twenty years old, Helen entered Radcliffe. While in college, Helen wrote an autobiography called *The Story of My Life.*

Helen dedicated the book to her friend Dr. Alexander Graham Bell.

In 1904, Helen Keller became the first person who was blind and deaf to graduate from an American college. With Anne's constant help, Helen graduated with honors.

Now, Helen was famous around the world. Mark Twain, the author of *Huckleberry Finn*, was her friend. She met movie stars and was even in a movie about her life.

Helen wrote books and articles for magazines. She gave speeches. To Helen, her own words sounded like a firing cannon. But to her audience, her voice was actually a whisper. So Anne would repeat Helen's words to the audience and Helen would be understood.

Helen worked hard to raise money for children who were blind and deaf. She raised money for the American Foundation for the Blind. Helen and Anne hired Polly Thompson to help them. Polly learned to use hand signs and read Braille. Polly helped Helen give speeches, too.

Then, in 1936, Anne Sullivan became ill.

Helen held the hand of her constant companion as Anne died. Helen and Anne had shared their lives for nearly fifty years. "The light, music, and the glory of life had been withdrawn," Helen wrote, when Anne died.

Polly stepped in to be Helen's companion. Helen missed Anne, but Polly now helped Helen do all that she wanted to. Helen barely slowed down. She wrote a book about Anne's life. She visited soldiers hurt during World War II. After the war, Helen worked to help people who were blind and deaf.

Helen's courage and determination were recognized around the world. She received awards from Japan, Brazil, and France. Over her long life, Helen met eleven presidents: Grover Cleveland, William McKinley, Theodore Roosevelt, William Howard Taft, Woodrow Wilson, Calvin Coolidge, Herbert Hoover, Franklin D. Roosevelt, Harry S. Truman, Dwight D. Eisenhower, and John F. Kennedy. In 1964, President Lyndon B. Johnson awarded Helen the highest honor in the United States, the Presidential Medal of

Freedom. Helen was too ill to receive the award in person, so she never met President Johnson.

Helen Keller lived until she was almost eighty-eight years old. She died on June 1, 1968.

Helen Keller was blind and deaf for most of her life. Yet she could read, write, and speak. She wrote books. She won awards. She helped thousands of people to have better lives. Helen Keller worked hard to live a complete life. She wouldn't let her disabilities prevent her from doing things. Who would have guessed all Helen Keller would accomplish when she was born on June 27, 1880?